Christianity Pure & Simple

—— Booklet Three ——

The

by
Dwight Longenecker

All booklets are published thanks to the
generous support of the members of the
Catholic Truth Society

CATHOLIC TRUTH SOCIETY
PUBLISHERS TO THE HOLY SEE

Contents

1. Jesus Keeps His Promise

Let's not mince words. Christians believe Jesus Christ rose from the dead. We believe this astounding twist in the plot really happened. It

 wasn't a make believe happy fairy tale ending. It was a unique, physical and historical event. It surprised everyone and changed the course of human history forever.

Jesus said he would be with his followers until the end of time. Obviously, if Jesus were dead he couldn't be with them. But if Jesus Christ is alive then his Spirit can continue to be with his followers. It was therefore through his victory over death that Jesus was able to release his Holy Spirit into the world.

Did Jesus rise from the dead? Many people simply can't believe it and honestly admit that they are not Christians. Others want to be Christian, but can't believe that the resurrection really happened. They attempt to 're-interpret' the resurrection event, and say, 'Jesus didn't physically rise from the dead. Instead, Jesus' memory continued to live within the lives of his followers.'

This is another way of saying that the resurrection is simply a beautiful idea. But if the resurrection didn't really happen, that idea has no meaning. Its like saying marriage is a beautiful thing, as long as you don't live together or make love. But if you don't live together and make love, then a marriage is not a marriage, and it is not even a beautiful idea, it is not anything at all.

For marriage to have meaning it has to be physical. Likewise for the resurrection to have meaning it had to have happened. After all, that's what resurrection *means*: someone rose from the dead never to die again. It's no good just pretending that it was a beautiful idea.

Did it really happen?
Stop for a moment and think it through. If Jesus Christ really rose from the dead, then it is literally the most important event in human history. We mustn't tiptoe around the claims of the early Christians. They were present at the events and they told us what they witnessed.

If we want to think about the important

questions in life, then we must take a serious look at the events recorded in the gospels. Even if the resurrection of Jesus sounds incredible, we must consider the possibility fair and square. It is vital to do so because if Jesus did not really rise from the dead, then he was only a good teacher, and if he is only a good teacher he does not have the power to deliver us from death.

Consider the story: The gospel writers go out of their way to make it clear that the resurrection of Jesus really happened. The gospels were written within the lifetime of eyewitnesses. They report that many people saw Jesus die on the cross, and that three days later the same people saw him walking and talking in their midst.

These eyewitnesses touched Jesus. They saw him eat food. They even put their fingers in his open wounds. Certain details of the story may have altered slightly in the telling, but because eyewitnesses were still living when the gospels were written, we can trust that the gospel writers did not invent the story. Neither did they exaggerate or distort the actual events to any great degree.

Jesus' followers ran from the empty tomb in terror. That shows us just how real, frightening and earth shattering an event this was. Would they have invented such an unbelievable story? In general terms, the more fantastic a story is, the more unlikely it is that people have made it up. The fact that these men and women were prepared to die for their version of events makes us conclude that something stupendous really did happen to them.

A world turned upside down

The disciples had their world turned upside down. Once they realised what it meant they were overwhelmed, and we should be too, for the resurrection means that history is changed forever.

Human history is changed because if Jesus rose from the dead, then in theory at least, the great enemy death, can be cheated at last. If the resurrection only means that 'Jesus continued to live in the memory of his followers', then victory over death is no more than a bright idea. If there is no victory over death, then the Christian faith is just another religious system of prayer and good works like all the others.

However, if Jesus really rose from the dead, then human history is transformed forever. If he conquered evil and death, maybe I can too. Furthermore, if evil and death can be defeated, then the whole world can be transformed by that same power.

The Christian faith is about that very possibility, and St Paul was so sure of this exciting possibility that he cried out, 'Death! Where is your sting? Grave where is your victory?'

Up up and away

After Jesus rose from the dead he continued to teach his twelve apostles. Jesus said that he had to go away, but promised that he would be with them until the end of time. To remain with them he would send a 'comforter' or 'the Spirit of Truth.' This Spirit would 'lead them into all truth' and 'teach them all things.' The Spirit of Truth would come to help them, but they needed human leadership too, so Jesus asked Peter, the leader of the apostles, to take on the leadership role.

After he rose from the dead, Jesus could not just live forever on this earth. If he remained on earth his enemies would have kept on trying to kill him. But if he just disappeared people would assume that he had wandered off to die someplace quietly. If he faded away or vanished from their sight they would conclude that Jesus hadn't risen from the dead physically, but they had simply seen a ghost.

Jesus had to go away, but to make it clear that he

had really physically risen from the dead, and that he was not going to die again, he had to go to the spiritual realm in a visibly physical way. Jesus therefore made sure that his followers saw him physically depart from this earth.

Forty days after he rose from the dead he took his apostles to a hill outside Jerusalem. He gave them his own authority and power and told them to continue his work. To confirm his promise Jesus said his Spirit would help them to do his work in the world. Then he rose up, and they watched him go from their sight.

Is it difficult to believe that Jesus rose up from earth to heaven? If you accept that Jesus is who he says he is (God in human form) then it makes sense that he would not be able to stay dead. It also follows that once he had risen from the dead, he would need to go away in a physical way.

Having Jesus disappear into a cloud sounds like a fantasy story, but how else could it have happened? We know that heaven is not a big golden city on the other side of the clouds. Heaven is a spiritual realm. But because Jesus had to be seen to move physically to the spiritual realm, the spiritual realm had to be located somewhere, and the sky is the best symbol we have for the spiritual realm.

But Jesus didn't leave this earth for heaven simply to tie up the loose ends of the story. His return to heaven was also the completion of his destiny. By going to heaven as a human being he opened up the way for us to follow. By returning to heaven he took his place in that realm as the victorious hero returning home.

The fire and wind come down

After Jesus went to the spiritual realm his followers waited in Jerusalem. The Bible says they prayed and worshipped together along with Mary, the Mother of Jesus and others who had witnessed the resurrection. The apostles (which means 'sent ones') were the ones Jesus had specially chosen, and Peter was their leader, just as Christ had requested.

While they waited the apostles remembered Jesus through the simple memorial meal as he had commanded them. When he had celebrated the ancient Jewish Passover feast with them just before his death, Jesus had said the bread was his body and the wine was his blood.

The apostles believed that, in a way beyond human understanding, the bread and wine really did become the body and blood of Christ. In this way Jesus was present with them in a real and powerful way just as he promised he would be. As they ate the sacred bread and drank the wine they became part of Christ and he became a part of them.

At this time - just over forty days after the Passover festival - the apostles, along with Jews from all around the world had gathered in Jerusalem for the Jewish festival called Pentecost. Pentecost marked the end of the Passover season and the beginning of the harvest season. Pentecost was also a celebration of God's revelation to Moses on Mount Sinai. At Sinai God's presence was manifested in an earthquake, wind and fire.

As a fulfilment of this event the apostles also experienced an astounding manifestation of God's presence. Suddenly as they were together there was the sound of a mighty wind and they saw flames of fire appear over the heads of the apostles and their followers.

The little group of Jesus' followers felt a surge of power within them. This overwhelming experience must have given them a spiritual high because it is recorded that they were reeling and falling over with the effects of this sudden supernatural infilling of the Holy Spirit - so much so that the observers joked that they were drunk.

Then Peter stood up and got everyone's attention. He said his friends weren't drunk, as it was only nine o'clock in the morning. Instead, they were filled with the Holy Spirit just as Jesus had promised.

Powerful preaching

Peter told the Jewish people gathered there about Jesus, who had been killed, but had risen again. He reminded them that many people had seen Jesus alive, and that Jesus had risen again because it was simply impossible for death to hold him. He quoted passages from the Jewish religious writings to show the Jews how Jesus had fulfilled their ancient prophecies. Then he declared that the resurrection proved that Jesus was exactly who he said he was - the Jewish Messiah - the anointed servant of God - the very Son of God.

Then Peter delivered the final thrust. He told the Jewish leaders that they had crucified their own Messiah. Many people were swayed by Peter's powerful preaching and asked what they had to do. He answered, 'Repent and be baptised in the name of Jesus Christ for the forgiveness of sins and you will receive the gift of the Holy Spirit.'

At that moment the essence of the Christian

religion became clear. Human beings may have killed the one who was sent to save them, but in doing so, he actually accomplished what he was sent for. Human evil may have been great, but God's love was greater. By allowing himself to be a victim of evil, Jesus Christ defeated evil and death forever, and was able to offer a share in his victory to all people.

Peter says that we are able to join ourselves with Christ's victory in three simple steps. First we have to realise that, even though part of us wants to do good, all of us have chosen the selfish way in life. We have hurt others and ourselves. If we had been there in Jerusalem that fateful week we probably would have consented to Jesus' death, or at least stood silent and done nothing about it. Once we realise that we are on the side of evil, we must be sorry for the fact.

The second step is to switch sides. We must decide to live life God's way, not our way. Furthermore, we must accept that it is through Jesus' death and resurrection that we have the power to make this decision and stick with it.

As a sign of our decision, we must be plunged into water while invoking God the Father, Jesus, his Son, and the Holy Spirit. By this physical action our inner decision to change is put into action. By this process we are washed clean spiritually and enter into Jesus' life. The wrong things we have done are forgiven, and we receive the Spirit that Jesus had promised. Through this threefold action the New Testament says we are 'born again' and given a fresh start in life as members of God's family.

Anyone can begin this process at any time. If you have understood this simple core of the Christian faith now, as you read this, then you can take the first two steps of being sorry and switching sides right now. All it takes is for you to speak to God, saying that you are sorry, that you believe Jesus Christ died and rose again for your sake, and that you want to switch sides. If you have already been baptised, then by making this decision you have claimed what was done for you in baptism. If you have not been baptised, then you need to search out your local Catholic Church and talk to a priest, who will help you take the next step.

Twelve timid men

Did the events of Pentecost really happen? There are similar stories of mighty winds, supernatural flames and people speaking in strange heavenly languages right down to the present day, but these supernatural, religious events are not the best evidence that something amazing occurred in Jerusalem that day.

Something stupendous must have happened because of the historical and human results. Before Pentecost, Peter was a coward. When Jesus was taken away Peter had denied that he knew Jesus. The other apostles weren't much better. They were confused, frightened, ordinary men who were unsure of themselves and unsure who Jesus really was.

What happened to transform these twelve timid men into religious leaders who spearheaded a movement that eventually challenged the Roman Empire and transformed human history? Peter was ready to run away, but in the end he led the first Christians to stand up courageously for the truth. What happened to turn Peter from a weak coward to a powerful and fearless world leader who would eventually go to Rome and lay down his life for his beliefs?

The resurrection and ascension of Jesus released the power that came down at Pentecost. The three events are dependent on each other. The same power that raised Jesus from the dead was suddenly available to transform ordinary people's lives. The religious experiences of people ever since that momentous day in Jerusalem have proved that weak, ordinary people really can be transformed by this resurrection force.

The word for this transformation is 'conversion.'

Peter's is just one example of a life transformed. There are countless others. Francis of Assisi was a confused young soldier home from the wars, but he was converted from a spoiled dreamer of a rich boy into the founder of a powerful religious movement that changed the world.

Mother Teresa was just an ordinary nun teaching in a convent school, but the same power that transformed Peter and Francis of Assisi turned her into a spiritual dynamo who established an international movement. She went on to challenge presidents and prime ministers with her message of the preciousness of human life.

The conversion experiences described in the New Testament are echoed in millions of ordinary lives down through history. The evidence of transformed lives is everywhere, and if it happened to Peter and Francis of Assisi and Mother Teresa, then it can happen to you and to me too.

A global vision

This is how Jesus planned to transform the whole world: by transforming individuals who would change the world. He said that a seed could not grow unless it falls into the ground and dies. He also said that his kingdom was like a tiny seed that is planted, then grows into a huge tree, full of life and power.

Jesus was the little seed that died and was buried. His resurrection was the growth and blossoming of that great tree. The gift of the Holy Spirit is like the life-giving sap in that tree. The whole family of Christ's followers down through the ages is like the tree that is growing to provide a place of shelter and shade for the whole world.

At Pentecost God's plan for the renewal and transformation of the world became clear. By his death and resurrection, Jesus Christ released a power into the world that would continue to work through the world as electrical current surges through an electricity system. This fresh life force is always there working to bring about new life; to rescue all that is soiled and dying, and bring it to a fresh, new beginning. Furthermore, the same creative Spirit that was released at Pentecost had been active from the beginning of time.

2. The Transforming Power of the Spirit

At Pentecost humanity experienced the spiritual equivalent of a huge volcano. Forces that had been bubbling beneath the surface suddenly burst out with enormous power. Before Pentecost God's Spirit was surging and working in the world, but in a more general way. When Jesus came, the work of the Spirit came into focus. When he died and rose again, Jesus released God's powerful Spirit into the world in a more specific way.

Because the Holy Spirit was at work in the world from the beginning it is worth looking to the past to see how and what he did. The Spirit's work is recorded in the Old Testament, which is the first half of the Bible. By seeing how the Holy Spirit worked in the Old Testament we can then understand how the Spirit is focussed in the life and teaching of Jesus Christ. Seeing this will then help us to understand how the Spirit can transform our lives today.

At the beginning of the Bible the Jewish people recorded their ancient creation story. They were not giving a scientific and historical account of the beginning of the world. Instead, in simple, poetic language they described how God was the source of all things from the beginning. In majestic words they said, 'In the beginning God created the heavens and the earth and the earth was without form. It was empty, and the breath of God moved over the surface of the deep watery chaos.'

Two pictures come together in these ancient words. One is the image of a great bird hovering over the watery chaos. That shadowy presence was there from the beginning as the creative power behind all things. The other image is of 'God's breath.' By breathing over the watery darkness God brought life into existence.

This 'hovering spirit' or 'breath of God' can also be understood as the 'Spirit of God.' In other words, God's Holy Spirit was there at the beginning, as the creative force in the world. Later in the creation story this same spirit brings man to life because God 'breathes into Adam the breath of life.'

Jesus and the creator spirit

At creation the Holy Spirit, like a great hovering bird, brought new life out of the waters of chaos. The same image is echoed when Jesus was baptised. When he came up out of the water he saw the Spirit like a dove hovering over him. The symbolism is the same: the Spirit is present to bring forth a new kind of spiritual life.

As the 'breath of God' brought creation into being, and breathed life into the first human, so after his resurrection, Jesus breathed on his apostles and said, 'Receive the Holy Spirit.' This is a symbol that they were being re-created, and that humanity was getting a fresh start with a new breath of God.

It is no coincidence that at Pentecost the followers of Jesus heard the sound of a mighty rushing wind. The creative breath that Jesus had blown on his apostles in a symbolic way was the same breath of God that had blown over the world at the beginning of creation. The same Spirit of new life is now available to breathe new life into our stale, confused existence. The Spirit that brought creation out of chaos is actively seeking to create order out of the chaos and confusion of our lives.

The spirit of liberty

The Spirit's character is revealed by what the Spirit does. In the Old Testament one of the things God's Spirit does is liberate slaves and deliver from death. The story of Exodus reveals how God's Spirit saved the Jewish people from death and brought them into freedom from their slavery in Egypt.

Moses was a young Jewish man who had been brought up in the court of the Egyptian pharaoh. After committing a murder he had to flee for his life into the wilderness. In the desert he married and began to live as a nomadic shepherd.

Then one day as he was tending his sheep Moses was startled by a vision of a bush on fire. When he looked closer he saw that although the bush was burning it was not being consumed by the flames.

Moses heard a voice that seemed to come from within the bush. The voice said that it was the God of his Jewish ancestors, and that Moses was destined to return to Egypt to lead the Jews out of slavery to freedom in their own land.

Eventually Moses obeyed. In Egypt the Spirit delivered the Jewish people from terrible plagues and a sure death. When they were finally released the Jewish people were led on their journeys by a cloud that was like a pillar of fire. The burning bush, and the cloudy pillar of fire were powerful symbols of the Holy Spirit. The fire brought light and warmth and led them into freedom.

Jesus and the fire of freedom

John the Baptist's message was also about freedom from slavery and death. He announced that someone greater than himself would soon appear. John said, 'I have baptised with water, but one is coming who will baptise you with the Holy Spirit and with fire.' Then Jesus appeared and was baptised by John.

Straight after his baptism Jesus went out into the desert where he went through a time of spiritual testing. Then he went to his home town Nazareth and announced his mission. He went into the synagogue (which was the local Jewish church) and read a passage from the Old Testament prophet Isaiah which said, 'The Spirit of the Lord is upon me, because he has anointed me to preach good news to the poor. He has sent me to proclaim release to the captives and recovering of sight to the blind, to set at liberty those who are oppressed.'

Everyone stared at him. What could he mean? The passage Jesus had read referred to the expected servant of God, the anointed one - the Messiah. Then to their amazement Jesus said with complete confidence, 'Today this prophecy is fulfilled in your hearing.' Just as the Holy Spirit had led the Jews out of slavery, Jesus claimed to have a special calling to do the same thing.

Jesus' ministry was only the start. When the tongues of fire appeared on the day of Pentecost, God was using the same symbol of fire to show that the Spirit who had liberated the Jewish people from slavery in Egypt was now given to deliver people from slavery to their twisted selfish nature.

Each one of us are enslaved to some sort of addiction or weakness. The fiery energy force that delivered the Jewish people is now available to us. The Holy Spirit can help to deliver us from the slavery of our addictions, our fears and our selfishness and lead us to a new spiritual life - a life that is abundant and free.

The spirit of wisdom

The Jewish people finally came into their Promised Land, and eventually a king was chosen to rule over them. King David consolidated the kingdom and established peace and prosperity. He was succeeded by his son Solomon.

During this time the different civilisations around Israel had started to write down 'quotable quotes' - wise sayings that helped people to get on in life. The Jewish people developed their own forms of wisdom literature. They added drama, poetry and stories to the quotable quotes to have memorable ways of passing their wisdom from one generation to the next. Solomon was considered the wisest king of the time because he was a master of this kind of practical wisdom.

Eventually the Jewish people came to understand that wisdom was not only practical advice for dealing with life's problems. If a person really wanted to be wise they would have to ask the big questions about life: Why are we here? Is there a God? Why must we die? How can God be good yet allow suffering?

The Jews realised that people cannot answer these questions on their own. The big questions are so difficult to answer, and there was so much disagreement, that the Jews realised they needed to have the truth revealed to them by a higher power. They visualised a 'Spirit of Wisdom' that led them to enlightenment and spiritual understanding.

Wisdom and wave-walking

When Jesus was a boy Luke tells us on two occasions that Jesus 'grew in wisdom'. Luke doesn't simply mean that Jesus was getting a good education. Luke understood from the Old Testament that 'wisdom' was another name for the Holy Spirit.

In the Old Testament 'wisdom' is a person. She is a wise woman who plays at the dawn of creation. If 'wisdom' is a person, then in Jesus' life we see that person guiding and leading him to such an extent that he actually performs the same actions as Wisdom.

There is an interesting detail from the gospel stories that illustrates what I mean. The Jewish thought of the sea as a dangerous and chaotic place. In some Old Testament passages God is the one who calms the sea and walks on the waves, and in one of the Old Testament wisdom poems it is Wisdom who 'walks on the waves of the sea.'

In the gospels Jesus calms a storm and in one story he actually comes to his followers by walking across the waves. These stories were not told simply to impress people with Jesus' ability to do miracles. The gospel writers told the stories to make people consider who Jesus really was.

The people who first heard these stories knew who had the power to calm the storm and walk on the waves. So when Jesus performed these powerful actions his followers rightly asked the question, 'Who is this man?'

They knew from the Old Testament that 'God is the one who brings creation out of watery chaos. God is the one who calms the storm, and it is the Holy Spirit of Wisdom who walks on the waves of the sea.' Since Jesus calmed the storm and walked on the waves, the first Christians concluded that Jesus was the Wisdom of God in human form.

When Jesus sent his Spirit onto individuals at Pentecost they realised that the same Spirit of Wisdom that had lead the ancient Jews to understand the Truth was also with them to lead and guide them into all truth. That same Spirit of Wisdom is available to each one of us. All we need to do is ask.

Tapping into the power

Throughout the history of the Jewish people the spirit of creation continued to bring them into new life. The same Spirit continued to lead them into freedom whenever they fell back into the slavery of selfish, destructive behaviour. Through their poets, priests and preachers the Spirit continued to teach them and bring them to new insights and understandings about themselves and God.

By the work of the Spirit the Jews were being prepared for the coming of Jesus, and through their history, God would open up the whole world to a fresh understanding of his goodness and truth. When Jesus came he did the same things in a specific way that the Holy Spirit had done within the history of the Jewish people.

Jesus brought new life. He said, 'I have come that you may have life in all its fullness.' Jesus also brought freedom. By healing people he delivered them from the bondage of ill health. By forgiving their sins he delivered them from guilt, fear and darkness. Jesus also taught them the truth about God, and so led them in the paths of real wisdom.

But Jesus was not just full of the Holy Spirit as any other religious leader might be. He was actually one with the Holy Spirit. Likewise, Jesus did not simply teach the people about God the Father. He said, 'I and the Father are one.'

In other words, Jesus is the connecting point between God and the Holy Spirit. He is also the junction point between us and God. This unity between Jesus, the Holy Spirit and God is vital because it shows us where we can get the power needed for our lives to be transformed.

Jesus does not just teach us about God and the Holy Spirit. He takes us into real, powerful contact with God. In order to understand how this happens we have to understand better how Jesus, God and the Holy Spirit live and work as one.

3. The Father, Son and Holy Spirit

Probably the most unusual and difficult belief that Christians hold is the idea that the one God consists of three persons: Father, Son and Holy Spirit.

Many people don't see what the fuss is all about. It makes sense to them that there is only one God. They quite rightly say that God is a total and utter mystery. God's real being is far beyond our powers of understanding or description. They wonder why we have to bother with such a difficult and seemingly contradictory concept as the Trinity.

One of the reasons we bother is because, as the first Christians began to think about the way God worked in the world they came to realise that Jesus actually acted like God in human form. They realised that Jesus did the things that, in the Old Testament, the Holy Spirit had done. It was by thinking about Jesus that they came to realise that he was one with the Spirit and the Father.

The resulting concept is difficult to understand intellectually, but if we try to put ourselves into the shoes of the first Christians we will see that this explanation about God's character fits best with the other things we know about God.

Despite the difficulties, the Trinity is the best way of understanding God. Furthermore, this understanding is not just a head game. This truth about God is practical. It really does help the other pieces of the puzzle fit into place. Understanding more of the Holy Trinity helps us to understand God better, but more importantly it helps us experience God better.

God talk

Since God is totally beyond our comprehension it is appropriate to use a mysterious concept to indicate what he is like. The Trinity itself is a mystery - that is to say, it is a truth we can experience, even if we cannot explain it. That sounds like gobbledegook, but when you think about it there is a very ordinary aspect of life where this is also true. Love is something we can experience but not explain. The Trinity is like that. We can experience it, but we cannot explain it.

The mystery of the Trinity has been explained with many different types of picture language. Saint

Patrick said it was like clover leaf - one leaf, but three leaves. Others have said it is like water - it takes three different forms - solid, liquid and gas, but all three are still water. All of these descriptions might help people understand the Trinity, but none of them are totally satisfactory. They can never be more than picture language to try to explain what is beyond our ability to understand.

One of the reasons none of these word pictures works completely is because all of them are just pictures. If God is Three in One, then we can't make a picture of him. This is because God the Three in One is as much about what God does as what he is. That is why some people say the three aspects to God are his three different ways of working in the world.

If Father, Son and Holy Spirit are three different ways that God works in the world, then the best term we have for these three different ways of working is 'persons'. We call the Father, Son and Holy Spirit 'persons' because like any person, they have distinct characteristics and ways of behaving.

The family God

If the three members of the Trinity are persons, then they don't expect us to study them, but to be in a relationship with them. You wouldn't consider a photograph of your family or a family history to be the same thing as being in a relationship with the real people. It's the same with God. None of the images we have of God are really good enough. God wants us to understand him better than that. He doesn't want us to simply have mental pictures of what he is like. He wants us to enter into a real relationship with him.

That is why the best way to speak of the Holy Trinity is to talk about family life. God's life is not empty and dead. Instead it is a dynamic loving relationship between three persons. The Father, the Son and the Holy Spirit are like a human family. As a man, woman and child are united as one through marriage, so that three way union of love reflects the reality of God himself.

If God is like a family, then at the core of God's life is love. This is the practical and astounding truth that is unlocked by the mystery of the Holy Trinity: that God is Love. If God is love, then we come to know God by learning more about love. We also experience the reality of the Trinity by experiencing the reality of God's love in our lives.

We learn best about love by being members of a family. That is why when we become Christians it is said that we are being adopted as God's children. This not only means that we enter the family of all other people who believe, but we enter the 'family' that is made up of Father, Son and Holy Spirit.

Welcome home

This is what Jesus came to accomplish. He broke down the barrier between God and humanity in order to welcome us into a relationship with his own father, God. Like an older brother, Jesus came into this world to seek and to save his lost brothers and sisters and bring them home.

We claim our family inheritance by realising we are cut off from God, deciding to switch sides and being baptised. Baptism is a ritual that brings about the truth it signifies. Being put into the water at baptism is a sign of being put into Christ's death. Rising up out of the water is a sign of rising up with Christ in his resurrection. In other words, through baptism we are being 'put into' Christ. We become one with Christ and he becomes one with us.

When Jesus was baptised the voice from heaven said, 'This is my beloved son' and the Holy Spirit descended like a dove. This was a picture that in baptism Father, Son and Holy Spirit are together as one, powerful, dynamic unit.

Therefore, when you become a Christian you are baptised not just in the name of Christ, but in the name of the Father, Son and Holy Spirit. This is because, through baptism we really do enter into a relationship with the God who is Father, Son and Holy Spirit.

Just as God said to Jesus, 'You are my beloved Son.' So at our baptism into Jesus Christ, God says to us, 'You are my beloved child.' Through this transaction we become part of God's family. God becomes our Father. Jesus becomes our Brother and the Holy Spirit enters our life to bring us right into the centre of that reality that is God himself.

Christ's life within us

If you have stayed with me thus far you will see that the Christian faith is not simply about obeying a set of religious rules and trying hard to be a good person. Christianity is far more radical than that.

Instead of a set of rules to obey, the Christian faith is about accepting God into the very core of our lives. When we are baptised, the life force of Jesus Christ enters our life and begins the life long process of transformation within us.

Father, Son and Holy Spirit exist in perfect unity. As Christ enters into our life he wants to create a new unity within us. Jesus prayed that his followers might 'be one as he and the father are one.' In other words, all the chaotic, divided parts of us are to be harmonised and work together in unity. Our body, our mind and our spirit are meant to work as one - not be divided against each other.

It is important to get a small glimpse of what the Holy Trinity means because then we come to realise the simple truth that as we accept Christ into our lives we are actually opening the very heart of our being to God himself. The three way God of Love is working in and through us to bring us to our final destiny. That destiny is nothing less than a life lived within the everlasting power and glory of God's own life of love.

Love binds them all together

Just as it is impossible to explain love it is impossible to explain the Trinity. But just as it is possible to know love by experiencing it, so it is possible to begin to understand the Trinity by experiencing God's powerful love.

By love I don't mean the sentimental stuff of romantic movies and love songs. They are fine, but I am talking about something far greater and far more mysterious and noble and tragic and true. The love I am talking about is the force that actually binds all things together.

The force that moves the sun and the other stars is the power of Love. Love is the outgoing, goodness of God in the universe. Love is also the power that binds the three persons of the Trinity together. Love attracts the Father, the Son and the Holy Spirit and binds them in a perfect harmony and unity like a great magnetic force.

This is the powerful love that we are called to share in. Love binds us together with one another, but it is also binds us into the very heart of the Trinity. We tap into that love and become a part of it as you might plug into an electric circuit.

All you need is love

To be a Christian therefore is not to try to be very good all the time. Instead being a Christian means learning to live and move within and through the power of Love. The New Testament says, 'those who live in Love live in God and God lives in them.' As we live a life of love for ourselves, for our families, for other people and for the world we are not just making the world a better, nicer place, but we are also joining ourselves with the energy that binds everything together in a perfect harmony.

The love of God is the energy force that draws us into relationship with him, but all of our lesser loves on earth are also part of that greater love. When we live in the love of a human family, when we engage in loving actions towards others, when we forgive and make time for others we do so within the greater love that binds God together, and which moves the sun and all the other stars.

Jesus Christ is the way for us to be bound into this wonderful energy supply called love. He shows us that love in its fullness and empowers us to live within that love more and more each day. Do you want to have a full and abundant life and make the world a better place? Do you want to find true love in this life, and a love that will last forever? Do you want to discover the secret of true happiness? Do you want to live life to the full and take hold of all that life has to offer with open arms?

Then open your life to this power of Love. It is available to all. It is not easy to claim it, for everything within us whispers that we should turn away from this Love. But if we give ourselves to this love and ask for the gift of this love, then it will most certainly be given and we will be able to begin the greatest adventure that life has to offer.

Down through the ages real, ordinary people have been transformed by the power of God's love in their lives. They have given themselves totally to this love and it has burned in their lives with such radiance and power that the whole world has seen that their lives have been transformed. How this amazing transformation can happen is the subject of the next chapter.

4. Going With God

For some time I have been talking about the power of transformation in our lives. It has been necessary to outline where that power comes from. I've done this because it is important to realise that we cannot change ourselves. The bookshops are full of self-help books. They contain much that is good and helpful, but there is a basic flaw in all of them. They don't put you in touch with a power greater than yourself.

Christians believe that God's Holy Spirit gives us an amazing power source for change in our lives. Because of Jesus Christ's death and resurrection that power source is available to every person who asks for it. This burning energy source is necessary if we really want to change for good.

To connect with this source is to connect our lives with the inner life of God himself. To open our lives to this power is to open up to the force called Love by whom all things were created, and by whom they continue to consist. It is easy to connect with this fire force, but the first and most important step is to realise that we *need* this power of change in our lives, and that we cannot change on our own.

Turning around

The reason self-help books sell so well is that we want to believe that we can change without the help of God. I'm sorry. We can't. We just don't have the power to change permanently on our own. Of course we can make improvements to our lives, but we cannot change the way we really are deep down inside.

There is only one power that can bring that kind of inner revolution, and that it the spiritual power unleashed by the Holy Spirit. The first step to receiving this power is to realise that we need it. This means we have to change our mind. We have to see, first of all, that we cannot change ourselves by ourselves. This means we have to experience a very fundamental shift in our attitude.

We do not need just an ordinary type of changed mind. Instead we need a radical re-alignment of our whole life. We need to see that we are headed in the wrong direction and decide to change course entirely.

Realising that we are on the wrong course is not the same thing as saying we are totally and utterly wrong in everything. It just means you have been building on sand when you should have been building on solid rock. It means we begin to say, 'I need help.'

Come down O love divine

Really admitting that we need help doesn't come easily. The conviction that we really are all right as we are dies hard. Sometimes we only come to a true reversal of our attitude because we have reached rock bottom in life. Through illness, bereavement, bad luck or our own stupid choices we come to the point where we have nowhere else to turn, and we realise then at the very deepest level of our personalities that we need help and only God can bail us out.

This ground level change of heart is not just admitting that in theory we need help, but *knowing* that we need help. Then we can really turn to God and ask for the Holy Spirit to come to our aid. At that point we are open to receive the gift of Divine Love or the gift of the Holy Spirit in a new way.

If we are not at rock bottom, but we still want to understand what this kind of change of heart is about then it is enough to ask for the gift of 'repentance.' Repentance is a technical word for this ground level shift of awareness. Then the Holy Spirit will actually help us to understand our deepest need in a more powerful way. Then, once we have realised our need, we are ready to receive the power to change.

Jesus Christ released that power in the world. All we need to do is acknowledge that fact and ask for his Spirit within our lives. He has promised to send that Spirit, and if we ask we will most certainly receive. If we seek he has promised that we will find the treasure. Trusting that he will give us the power to change is called 'faith'.

Teamwork required

Having repentance and faith is not a once and done thing. It is true that we need to come to a set time when we really do turn towards God for good, but we also need to check our spiritual compass daily. Day by day we need to check whether we are aware of our need for God and if we are living in faith.

Living this way is an adventure. It means new possibilities open up because God is in charge now, not us. Those who live by faith are on a journey into a new and unknown land - a land that promises to be full of new riches as well as new challenges.

Living in repentance and faith opens us up to God's marvellous way of working in the world. Suddenly we can see that someone else is working in and through our lives to transform us into all that we can be. Furthermore, he is working through us to change the world. We realise that we have become his agent in the world, and that if we stay with him fantastic and wonderful things can happen.

To stay in this state of repentance and faith we must work with the Holy Spirit. The help that God gives us, first to understand him and then to turn towards him regularly is called "grace". Living in a 'state of grace' means that we dwell constantly in an awareness that we need God, and that he is always by our side.

The great challenge
God helps us to see our need and turn towards him, but we must always remember that God will not override our will. He will not force us to love him. If he did, the result would not be love. For love to be real we must choose to turn from our own way and follow Gods way.

God gives us the power to choose, but we must use that power. God's help is available to everyone. All we need to do is ask, and the Holy Spirit will help us. We then have to act within that power in order to be transformed

The work of total transformation is not easy or quick. In fact you will find that trying to follow God's way is the hardest thing you have ever done. Those of us who are trying to follow this path admit that we often get confused and lose our way. Many times we stumble and fall on the path to perfection. What matters is not how often we fall, but how often we get up.

The sign that the Holy Spirit is at work in our lives is that we can see new powers developing in our lives. A new order grows within us; certain abilities that were lying dormant suddenly start to develop; in many practical ways our lives begin to change. The Spirit gives these new powers to help us grow as people and to better understand God's ways and wisdom.

The gifts of the Holy Spirit

The gifts of the Holy Spirit are actually supernatural gifts. They are qualities of mind, intelligence and Spirit that help us to grow into all that God created us to be. Although they are supernatural gifts, they are expressed and worked out in our lives in seemingly natural ways.

The Holy Spirit gives a whole range of different new abilities, but there are seven recognised gifts that we can notice becoming active in people's lives. The first of the seven gifts of the Holy Spirit is wisdom. Wisdom was the power of God that helped to make all things. In our lives wisdom is the ability to apply the spiritual insights we have received to our practical circumstances. Wisdom helps us to see clearly; to get our priorities right and grow in understanding.

Understanding is the second gift of the Holy Spirit. It is not easy to understand spiritual matters. Our eyes are darkened, but the Holy Spirit has been given to teach us all things. As we learn more about our faith the Holy Spirit is there as our teacher and mentor. With the gift of understanding our range of interests changes. We discover that we are more and more interested in spiritual things.

It is difficult to know the right way through life. We are often faced with difficult decisions. As we learn to listen to the Holy Spirit in our lives these decisions become easier. We are able to see the right way and discern what is best. The ability to discern what is right and wrong and understand which spiritual things are true and false is called 'counsel' and is the third gift of the Spirit.

The fourth gift is 'fortitude'. This is the supernatural strength to do what is right. When we are faced with a temptation, if we ask the Holy Spirit for help it will be there. In practical terms 'fortitude' helps us to stand up for what is right.

Knowledge is another gift of the Holy Spirit. This is not just head knowledge, but a real experience of spiritual truths. This kind of knowledge of life is the kind you have by being in love, not the kind you get from reading love poems. The spiritual gift of knowledge is not purely intellectual. It is practical and useful. With this kind of knowledge we can help others to know the truth and live by it.

'Piety' is the gift to live the spiritual life in all naturalness and goodness. This is not us trying hard to be holy and good, but the supernatural ability to be holy and good naturally. A truly 'pious' person does try hard to be good, but eventually the Spirit brings him to a place where he does good naturally. This is like an athlete who trains hard, but then wins the race with ease and a sense of exhilaration.

The last gift is 'fear of the Lord'. This does not mean that we tremble in constant fear in the face of God. Instead it means that we live in a state of repentance and faith. 'Fear of the Lord' is a constant joyful awareness that we need God and that he is with us always.

5. Total Transformation

When the Holy Spirit begins to work in someone's life it is as if they are a new person. The old things have passed away, and all things have become new. Not only do they see themselves in a

new away, but they see everyone else in a new light too. Indeed they see the whole world in a new way.

As we live in the Spirit other people will begin to see that there is something different about us. Perhaps they can't define it, but they realise that our priorities have changed.

The Holy Spirit has given us a new way of seeing, and a new way of being.

Of course the new person is not made perfect immediately. We have to work hard with God for the Holy Spirit to really take control of our lives. But eventually we find that our old habits are replaced by new ways of thinking and behaving. Bit by bit in our daily lives we find that change really is taking place. We really *are* becoming more patient with our children, our difficult family members or that awkward person at work.

The Spirit works within our ordinary lives to give them an extraordinary wealth of meaning, purpose and power. This process of perfection is gradual and natural. Like the growth of a great tree, it takes time for the roots to go deep. It takes time for the branches to grow and for the fruit to ripen, but when the fruit is ripe everyone benefits.

Likewise, the Spirit brings to fruition certain recognisable traits within the spiritual person. These characteristics are called the fruits of the Holy Spirit. The fruits of the Holy Spirit are developed by the supernatural work of the Spirit. Although the Spirit is supernatural his work is not un-natural. The fruits of the Spirit are the best of our human character brought to full development by the Spirit's power.

The fruits of life

The first fruit is 'charity'. Charity is not just an organisation that helps poor people. Neither is charity simply doing good to others. Instead it is an inner quality. Charity is that personality trait in which one loves and accepts others exactly as they are. In our daily lives 'charity' means we become naturally more patient and tolerant because deep down we really have come to desire the best for others - not just for ourselves.

Joy is the second fruit that the Spirit helps to ripen in our lives. Joy is not just happiness or fun. Instead Christian joy is a supernatural kind of happiness. Joy is marked by a special spiritual energy and enthusiasm for life. The Spirit brings joy because the person can see that an all-loving God is at work in the world. Because of this they really can see the positive side of every problem.

Joy is linked with the third fruit: peace. The Bible talks about 'the peace that passes all understanding' and Jesus said to his disciples, 'I give you peace. Not peace as the world gives.' the person who lives in the power of the Holy Spirit knows a deep peace despite things going wrong. The Spirit-filled person has peace because she knows that God is in charge, and in the end all shall be well.

Along with inner peace and charity comes patience and kindness. For a Christian patience and kindness are not simply a matter of being polite and having good manners. Instead the person who is filled with the Holy Spirit is patient and kind not because they are trying to be, but because genuine patience and kindness have become part of their nature.

It is the same thing with the other fruits of the Spirit. A person is good, and generous, gentle, faithful and modest not so much because they are trying hard to be that way, but because their nature has been transformed, and they have become all that they were first created to be.

Becoming sons and daughters of God

This is the exciting destination for all people. We really are destined to be the sons and daughters of God - brothers and sisters of Christ. Over and over again throughout the writings of the New Testament, and in the lives and writings of all the Christian saints we are called not to a life of religious rules and regulations, but a life that is transformed by the power of God.

Religion has become irrelevant and meaningless to many people because of this fundamental mistake. They have misunderstood the most important thing. Jesus did not come to enforce a great list of rules. The Christian faith is not first and foremost, a religion of respectability and good manners. It is a religion that fills, transforms and glorifies individual human beings.

Of course this is not easy, but Therese of Lisieux calls us to the challenge with youthful zeal, 'You cannot be half a Saint,' she cries, 'you must be a whole Saint, or no Saint at all!" A saint, is not simply a pious goody goody type of person. The saints are brave, idealistic, unyielding and totally devoted people. They are the spiritual equivalents of world champion mountain climbers. The saints are utterly committed to their beliefs. They love God with all their heart, mind and strength.

In doing so, they show us the possibility of total transformation into radiant and powerful people. This is what Christianity is about, no less than the total transformation of our lives into all that we were created to be - and what we are created to be are sons and daughters of the living God.

Change the world (and start with yourself)

Not only are we called to be totally converted ourselves, but as this action takes place in our lives, it is also happening in the lives of millions of other people all over the world. The work of the Holy Spirit down through the ages is to convert not just individuals to the will of God, but to bring the whole world back into relationship with God.

Do you want to change the world? Begin by changing yourself. The most efficient and powerful way to change yourself is to use the power of the person who made you. As the Holy Spirit transforms our lives we begin to fit into God's plan for the whole world. We become part of a world wide movement that is changing the course of history.

The study of history shows that it is the religious ideas of individuals and nations that motivate the transformation of history. Believers transform the world. Unbelievers cannot even transform themselves. As we believe, so we will do, and if we believe the Holy Spirit will transform our lives we can be part of his action in the world.

There is a group of people in the world who have given themselves to have this very action. This international group of believers are all empowered by the Holy Spirit. All of them are all working together with the spirit as much as they can. Before Jesus left this earth he not only gave his Holy Spirit to his followers, but he also told his followers to form a community of all those who were filled with his Holy Spirit. This little group of Holy Spirit people has grown for the last two thousand years. It now exists in every country of the world and it is growing faster and more powerfully than ever before. This group of people is called the Church.

6. The People of God

From the very beginning God began his work on earth within a family. The Jewish writers were keen to show that they had descended from their father Abraham, and that he had descended from Adam and Eve. In other words, the special relationship that God established with Adam and Eve continued down through the generations.

The Old Testament is the story not just of Spirit-filled individuals like Abraham, Moses, Joshua, David and the prophets. It is also the story of a Spirit-filled tribe called the Jews. Throughout the Old Testament God is concerned with the whole family of Abraham - not just with certain individuals.

This shows God's way of working in the world. He works through a chosen group of people. God's Spirit fills the individuals in that family, but the Spirit also directs the whole people of God. God works in the world both through individuals and through a whole body of faithful people.

The church is the family of Christ

The same Holy Spirit that filled, renewed, guided and taught the Old Testament people of God was given to the followers of Jesus at Pentecost. By doing this a new kind of spiritual family was established. Because each individual has a share in the same spirit there is a family bond between them. Jesus said that each one is his brother or sister. He said, 'the one who does the will of my father is my brother or my sister.'

If each person who receives the Holy Spirit is a brother or sister of Jesus, then they are also the brother and sister of each other. Because they share in the same spirit they are members of the same family. This is not just a symbol or a way of speaking. This is a reality. Through the Holy Spirit every other Christian really is my spiritual brother or sister.

The Church, therefore is not simply a collection of like-minded people. A political party, a sports club, a charity or a pressure group - all of these are organisations of people with the same goal and the same interests. The Church, on the other hand, is more than that. It is a family.

If the people of God are a family, then it is impossible for someone to be Spirit-filled and not be a member of that family. Whether they like it or not, those who belong to God's family are members of this great family of God.

The Church as the body of Christ

The Church is a family, but the New Testament uses another image to talk about the people of God. It says that the Church is 'the body of Christ'. Each member of the church is like a cell in the body. As such every member is dependent on every other member, they cannot exist on their own.

Again, this is not simply a poetic way of speaking. In a very real sense the Church is Christ's body alive here on earth today. The body of all people who believe in Christ do his work in the world.

Those who are alive in the Spirit are alive to one another. The Spirit is constantly at work keeping all the Spirit-filled people working together in harmony like members of a vast orchestra. In this way, all the individual Christians do what they can do best, but at the same time they are working together with one another to accomplish Christ's plan of world transformation.

If the Church is the body of Christ, then we would expect the Church to show Christ at work in the world today. This is exactly what we do find. In earlier chapters we saw how the Spirit brings new life, freedom and understanding. Then we saw that Jesus did that same work when he was on earth.

Now he does this work through the ministry of the Spirit-filled people of God.

The body of Christ brings new life

One of the things the Holy Spirit does is to bring new life. The Holy Spirit was there at the beginning of creation bringing life out of the dark watery chaos.

Jesus breathed new life into his followers after his resurrection, and he linked this new life with the symbol of water. One night he said to a religious leader, 'You must be born again of water and the spirit.'

I will discuss this more later, but it is enough to say at this point, that through the Church we receive the gift of baptism. By being plunged into water, God brings us into a new kind of spiritual life. We receive the gift of the Holy Spirit, but we do so through the ministry of God's people on earth: the Church.

The Church is at work in the world bringing about new life in all sorts of ways. Through education, healing ministries, health care, political involvement, pastoral care and spiritual teaching Christ's body the Church continues to do his work of bringing new life to a dark, chaotic world.

If we have committed ourselves to live in the Spirit, then we have our work cut out for us. It is part of our mission and work to help bring new life to others, and to help renew the whole world with God's new life.

The body of Christ brings freedom

The Spirit brought freedom. Jesus brought freedom. The Church does the same work. Through forgiveness Jesus set people free to live a new kind of life, and in the Gospels Jesus gave his apostles authority to forgive sins in his name.

Jesus said, "as the Father has sent me so I am sending you." This authority to forgive sins was passed down from the first apostles to the Church leaders who came after them and that same authority can be found in the Church today.

In a later booklet we will discuss this in more detail. Now, it is enough to say that it is through the ministry of the Church that the power of Jesus to forgive and set free is most fully realised in our lives.

In all sorts of other ways the Church is also busy bringing the freedom of Jesus to the world. By political involvement, through charity work, writing and campaigning Christians are working to bring freedom, peace and justice to the world.

The Spirit, therefore, is not just our private gift. The Spirit should lead each one of us to work with our brothers and sisters to bring freedom, justice and peace to everyone.

The Church teaches with power

In the Old Testament the Holy Spirit taught the people the truth about God. Jesus was the truth about God, and his body on earth (the Church) continues the essential work of teaching people the truth.

When Jesus was on earth the people were amazed because he taught the truth with authority. This authority to know and teach the truth is something else Jesus shared with his apostles before he went back to heaven. He said, 'all authority on heaven and on earth has been given to me, go therefore and teach all nations, baptising them in the name of the Father, the Son and the Holy Spirit.

In other words, Jesus was not only telling his apostles to go out into the world and preach the gospel, he was also giving them the authority to do what he asked them to do. This is very important. There are many religious teachers in the world. How do we know which ones are right?

Again, I will say more about this in a later booklet, but it is enough to say that, through the power of the Holy Spirit, the Church down through the ages has continued to teach the truth with the same authority of Jesus. If we want to understand the truth about God most fully, then we look to Christ, and the Body of Christ here on earth is the community of Spirit-filled people that he established.

Not only does the Body of Christ help us to understand the truth about God, but the Spirit that fills the Church also helps us share that truth with others. If we are Spirit-filled people, then this is part of our way of working with the Spirit of Christ in the world.

Getting ready for the great battle

Once we have accepted the Holy Spirit into our lives we have not got to the end of the journey, we have only just started. The Christian life is an exciting journey. It is a pilgrimage to a glorious destination.

The Spirit-filled life is an adventure and challenge, but luckily we do not travel alone. We travel with a whole group of friends and family. In fact, it is impossible for us to travel this journey alone. By the simple fact that we are all joined to the same body of Christ we are invisibly connected with everyone else who is travelling the same journey.

It's a good thing we do not travel alone because the journey is difficult. There are many hardships on the journey, there are enemies who wish to attack us.

We struggle against the dark side of our nature and we struggle against the dark forces arrayed against us.

If we decide to go on this journey and join in with this battle, then God will be with us. He gives us training for warfare. He also gives us weapons for the battle, food for the journey and an army to battle with us. Most of all he not only gives us the weapons for the battle, but the power to use those weapons.

The fourth booklet in this series, *The Great Battle - Living by Faith,* will tell you how to join in the battle. It tells you where to find help. It tells you how God enables you to fight the battle. And it tells you how, through the power of the Holy Spirit, you can fight the good fight, finish the course and lay hold of the great prize that has been prepared for you.

Additional Reading

The Holy Bible - try and obtain a Catholic Edition or one which contains the 'Apocrypha'. The Jerusalem Bible or New Revised Standard Versions are good translations.

The four *Gospels* are also available from CTS at only £1.00 each.

The Catechism of the Catholic Church

Christian Classics
Mere Christianity by C.S. Lewis
The Screwtape Letters by C.S. Lewis
Orthodoxy by G.K. Chesterton
The Everlasting Man by G.K. Chesterton
The Creed in Slow Motion by Ronald Knox
Early Christian Writings by Maxwell Staniforth
The Penguin Dictionary of Saints by Donald Attwater and Catherine Rachel Jones

Modern Catholic Books
Catholocism for Dummies by J Trigilio and K Brighenti. 'For Dummies' is a highly successful series in plain English, without being patronising or simplistic.

Catholic Lives by Greg Watts - a collection of stories of people who have become Catholic.

The Path to Rome by Dwight Longenecker - a more weighty collection of conversion stories than *Catholic Lives*.

More Christianity by Dwight Longenecker - this book explains the Catholic faith in a friendly way to non-Catholic Christians.

Adventures in Orthodoxy by Dwight Longenecker - a witty and colourful exploration of Christian belief.

Exploring the Catholic Church by Marcellino D'Ambrosio - a good small introduction to the Catholic Church today.

What Catholics Really Believe by Karl Keating - exploration of the Catholic faith in a question and answer format.

Knowing the Real Jesus by David Mills - a well written exploration of what the first Christians thought about Jesus Christ.

Surprised by Truth by Patrick Madrid - three volumes of American conversion stories.

Where is that in the Bible? and *Where is that in Tradition?* by Patrick Madrid - easy to read Catholic answers written in a punchy style.

What to do next...

You can order one or all of the other books in the CTS Christianity Pure & Simple series:

1. Is Anybody There? (Ref Do 699)

2. The God Man (Ref Do 700)

3. The Fire Of Life (Ref Do 701)

4. The Great Battle (Ref Do 702)

5. Welcome Home (Ref Do 703)

The quickest way to order is to call CTS direct on 020 7640 0042

You can send us a fax if you wish, on 020 7640 0046

Or pop your order in the post to:
CTS, 40-46 Harleyford Road,
Vauxhall, London SE11 5AY

Or visit our website
www.cts-online.org.uk/pureandsimple.htm

If this book has interested you and you want to discover more about Christianity then you may also find useful the following list of organisations:

www.faithcafe.org

If perhaps you already have some familiarity with the Catholic Church, but would like to explore some of the themes you've read about in this series, your local church may run Catholic Faith Exploration or CaFE

Catholic Enquiry Office

For enquiries about becoming a Catholic, knowing more about the Church or finding your local parish church. 114 West Heath Road, London NW3 7TX; Tel: 020 8458 3316; Email: ceo@cms.org.uk